Warsaw, Poland, before World War II

For children everywhere —T.B.

"My life was difficult but interesting. That's the life I asked God for when I was young: God, give me a hard life, but make it beautiful, rich, and noble." —Janusz Korczak, *Ghetto Diary* *

* Quotes attributed to Korczak have been translated by the author from their Polish sources.

Copyright © 2009 by Tomek Bogacki

All rights reserved

Distributed in Canada by Douglas & McIntyre Ltd.

Color separations by Chroma Graphics PTE Ltd.

Printed in February 2009 in China by South China Printing Co. Ltd.,

Dongguan City, Guangdong Province

Designed by Irene Metaxatos

First edition, 2009

1 3 5 7 9 10 8 6 4 2

www.fsgkidsbooks.com

Library of Congress Cataloging-in-Publication Data

Bogacki, Tomasz.

The champion of children : the story of Janusz Korczak / Tomek Bogacki.— 1st ed.

p. cm.

ISBN-13: 978-0-374-34136-7

ISBN-10: 0-374-34136-2

1. Korczak, Janusz, 1878–1942. 2. Jews—Poland—Biography—Juvenile literature.

3. Holocaust, Jewish (1939–1945)—Poland—Biography—Juvenile literature. 4. Poland—Biography—Juvenile literature. I. Title. II. Title: Story of Janusz Korczak.

DS134.72.K67B64 2009

940.53'18092—dc22

[B]

2008016188

THE CHAMPION OF
CHILDREN

The Story of Janusz Korczak

Tomek Bogacki

Frances Foster Books   Farrar Straus Giroux   New York

On a rainy day in 1889, a boy wandered the streets of the Old Town in Warsaw, Poland. The people he saw were very poor, and they all looked hungry. Many of them were homeless children dressed in rags. The boy wished he could do something to help them. If he were king—and he imagined himself on a white horse—he would create a better world for these children, a world where no one suffered.

This is the story of Janusz Korczak, a remarkable man who dedicated his life to helping children.

Janusz Korczak was born Henryk Goldszmit in Warsaw in 1878. But we shall call him by his pen name, Janusz Korczak, for that is how he is known today. Janusz grew up in a comfortable home near the Royal Castle of Warsaw, where he was loved and well cared for. He played by himself for hours on end, building imaginary kingdoms out of blocks and waging wars to defend the rights of children. His parents worried that he lived too much in his imagination.

Only his grandmother really understood him. Janusz told her about his dream of changing the world. He told her he would throw away all money so there wouldn't be any poor or hungry children, like those he saw everywhere and was not allowed to play with. His grandmother called him a philosopher.

When Janusz was five years old, he learned that being Jewish set him apart in some way. His canary had died, and Janusz and his sister were going to bury it under a tree in the courtyard.

Janusz wanted to mark its grave with a cross, like those in the Catholic cemetery—so the canary could go to heaven, he thought. But the housemaid told him a bird was too lowly for a cross, and the janitor's son said the canary was Jewish so couldn't get into heaven anyway. Janusz wondered about this.

As a child, Janusz went with his nanny and younger sister to Saxon Garden, where he liked to feed the sparrows and have serious conversations with the men who gathered there.

His father took him on long walks by the river, where they
watched people who had to work very hard for a living.

They also went to the Old Town in Warsaw, where so many of
the poorest people lived, and Janusz saw for the first time how
difficult the children's lives were.

But at school, life was difficult for Janusz, too.
He had to speak Russian because Warsaw was annexed to Russia
at the time. Schoolchildren had no rights and were severely
punished, even beaten, for the slightest misstep. No one questioned
this treatment. But in his heart, Janusz knew it was wrong.

When Janusz was eleven years old, his life changed dramatically. His beloved father became sick and was unable to work. Seven years later, he died. Janusz started tutoring other students to help support the family. Seeing his own family struggle made Janusz even more determined to help the many children in Warsaw who had so much less than he did. He took food to the children of the Old Town and tried to give them hope. His dream of improving their lives had not faded.

By the time Janusz was ready for the university, he knew that he would devote his life to helping children. He studied medicine.

But his plans were interrupted by the Russo-Japanese War. This was the first of three wars in which he served as a medical doctor. He treated not only wounded soldiers but also children who were war casualties, and he saw firsthand how different real war was from the play wars he had imagined as a child.

After the war, Janusz worked in a hospital for Jewish children during the day and in the evening treated the children of poor families for free.

And when he returned home, late at night, he wrote, using Janusz Korczak as his pen name. In articles and books, he put forth his ideas about education and orphanages. He soon became well known as a doctor, a writer, and an advocate for children's rights.

When the Orphans Aid Society asked him to be the director of a new orphanage for Jewish children, Korczak quickly accepted. He wanted to do more than make children well—he wanted to change their lives. So he gave up his medical practice to start the orphanage.

He traveled to Paris, Berlin, and London to learn more about orphanages. Then he worked closely with the architects to design the place that he saw so clearly in his imagination, a place where children would thrive.

In 1912, the building at 92 Krochmalna Street was finished. Janusz Korczak and Stefania Wilczynska, who would run the orphanage with him, were there to welcome the children.

Korczak's idea was to let the children govern themselves. They elected a parliament to create the rules that everyone, including Korczak and his staff, had to follow.

A children's court, run by the children, decided on punishments if a rule was broken. The most important rule was that of forgiveness, and Korczak taught them that making a mistake was sometimes the best way to learn not to make it again.

There was a weekly newspaper, which everyone contributed to—children, teachers, friends of the orphanage, and Korczak himself. On Saturdays, after breakfast, the children gathered around Korczak to discuss the week's events and problems.

When new children entered the orphanage, they were each assigned an older child to help them for the first three months, like a parent or guardian. In time, the new child would be ready to help another newcomer. Korczak thought of it as forming a very big family. The children learned how to be self-sufficient and caring in this atmosphere of love and respect.

Once a week, they were weighed and measured and then
bathed, a new experience for some of them.

Friday nights were special as they celebrated the Jewish
Sabbath in the beautiful dining room where they also played
games, read, and did their homework.

Later, in their dormitories, Korczak told them stories and fairy tales, like "Puss in Boots," which taught them that life was full of surprises and anything was possible.

Running an orphanage was a huge responsibility, but Korczak always found time to spend with the children. He taught them useful skills, like sewing and carpentry, but he also liked to joke and play games with them.

Every summer, the entire orphanage went to their summer camp in the countryside. There, the children worked in the vegetable garden, swam and played sports, and hiked in the forest. Korczak believed that recreation was as important to their growth and development as education was.

The orphanage on Krochmalna Street was so admired that
Korczak was asked to help create another orphanage, for the
children of Polish workers, which he would co-direct with
Maryna Falska and run with the same system of self-government
as the orphanage for Jewish children. It was designed in the
shape of an airplane and was called Our Home.

Korczak started *The Little Review*, a newspaper that was
managed by children, and children from all over Poland were
invited to contribute to it. He also hosted a radio program to help
children deal with everyday problems. "When your mother or
father wants to spank you," he once suggested, "ask them to wait
half an hour, and most likely they will have changed their mind."

Late at night, after all the children were asleep, Korczak climbed the stairs to his attic room on Krochmalna Street to write. He wrote books for children and books about children for adults. This is where *King Matt the First*, his most famous children's book, was written.

The world outside the orphanages was changing. In 1939, Germany invaded Poland, and World War II began. During the first days of the war, Korczak was asked to go on the radio to offer encouragement to adults and children.

The Nazis soon decreed that all Jews were to be relocated to a walled Jewish quarter. Korczak and the children had to leave their comfortable home on Krochmalna Street and move to the ghetto.

Thousands of Jews were crowded into the ghetto,
separated by a brick wall from the rest of the city.

All Jews were required to wear white armbands with a blue
Star of David. Korczak risked arrest by refusing to wear one.

Korczak tried to establish the same routines in the orphanage's cramped ghetto home, but conditions were very primitive. There were almost twice as many children as on Krochmalna Street, now living in one crowded room divided into separate eating and sleeping areas.

But still, even during this difficult time, Korczak insisted on giving the children as much love and attention as possible and organized concerts and theater performances. From his private space carved out in the middle of the room, he could watch over the children while they slept. It was here that he wrote his famous *Ghetto Diary*.

The children were
still weighed and
measured each week.
But there was not
enough food, so day
after day they became
thinner and weaker.

Korczak walked around the ghetto, looking wherever he could for food and money and medicine for the children. He picked up anything that could be used for firewood to heat their space. And if he found ghetto children needing shelter, he took them in.

Many friends offered to help Korczak escape from the ghetto, but he refused to leave his children.

Two years later, the Nazis began to send people from the ghetto to concentration camps. And on August 6, 1942, Korczak was ordered to take the children to the train station. He led them out of the ghetto in a quiet procession.

Bystanders remarked on the children's dignity and poise, not fully understanding that they marched in peace because Janusz Korczak was with them, and with him the children always felt safe.

Korczak died with his children in the Treblinka extermination camp, but his spirit survives in all he achieved during a lifetime devoted to defending children. Though he couldn't save his orphans from the horror of the Holocaust, his insistence that children have the right to be loved, educated, and protected has continued to inspire people all over the world.

In honor of Korczak's work, the United Nations declared 1979 the International Year of the Child. The United Nations Convention on the Rights of the Child, created in 1989, was strongly influenced by Korczak's theories.

HISTORICAL NOTE

The border of independent Poland in the years between World War I and World War II, superimposed on a map of partitioned Poland during the late nineteenth century

At the time of Janusz Korczak's birth in 1878, the area that we now know as Poland was governed by Austria-Hungary, Russia, and the German Empire. Part of this area, sometimes referred to as the Kingdom of Poland (indicated in pink on the map), included the capital city of Warsaw and was annexed to Russia. In 1918, after more than one hundred years of being occupied by neighboring countries, Poland became independent. It remained so until the German occupation began in 1939.

AUTHOR'S NOTE

In the introduction to his best-known children's book, *King Matt the First*, Janusz Korczak wrote that when he was a young boy he wanted to be like King Matt, a reformer who would wage wars to create a better world for children and fight for their rights.

I was born in Poland during the Cold War, and I first heard about this heroic man from my grandmother when I was nine years old. Although World War II had ended fourteen years earlier, it was hauntingly present in Polish people's memories, and I often felt that we were still living in that time.

My grandfather was born the same year as Janusz Korczak. Like Korczak, he had to speak Russian in school. He also became a doctor, as Korczak did, and served in World Wars I and II.

After my grandmother told me about Janusz Korczak, I read *King Matt the First* and began to think not only about children's rights but about everybody's rights. In a Communist country, rights and privileges were given only to members of the Communist Party. This helped me understand Korczak's life under tsarist Russia's domination and his determination to empower children. Later, I read everything I could find by and about Janusz Korczak.

SOURCES
AND ACKNOWLEDGMENTS

I would like to thank Frances Foster for her unwavering support, patience, and creative editing. Without her, this book would not have been possible.

My main source for this book was Korczak's famous *Ghetto Diary*, written during the final months of his life.

An important source of factual information were the works of Igor Newerly, a Polish novelist and Korczak's secretary, among them his beautifully written *Rozmowa w sadzie piatego sierpnia: O chlopcu z bardzo starej fotografii* (Conversation in the Orchard on August Fifth: About the Boy from a Very Old Photograph), published by Czytelnik, 1978.

I am very grateful for conversations with Igor Newerly's son, Jaroslaw Abramow-Newerly, who knew Korczak personally and has been generous with his memories. My thanks also to Marta Ciesielska from the Korczakianum in Warsaw for providing materials and information about Korczak's life.

Also important were the many volumes of *Korczak's Complete Works*, published in Poland; Betty Jean Lifton's very rich biography of Korczak, *The King of Children: The Life and Death of Janusz Korczak* (Farrar, Straus and Giroux, 1988); and Andrzej Wajda's 1990 movie *Korczak* (in Polish).

I found inspiration for the illustrations in many places. Some of the scenes from Korczak's childhood were inspired by old paintings like *Sanders* by Aleksander Gierymski, painted around the time of Korczak's birth, and *Views of Warsaw* by Bernardo Bellotto (Canaletto). I saw many photographs from Korczak's life, walked through the streets of the Old Town in Warsaw, and visited the orphanage on Krochmalna Street (now Jaktorowska Street), which is still an orphanage and has been renamed after Janusz Korczak. His statue now stands in front of the building.

Warsaw, Poland, in 1945, after World War II

amazon.com

Details for Order #104-8687455-7530619
Print this page for your records.

Order Placed: November 5, 2009
Amazon.com order number: 104-8687455-7530619
Order Total: $33.56

Not Yet Shipped

Items Ordered	Price
2 of: *The Champion of Children: The Story of Janusz Korczak*, Tomek Bogacki Condition: New Sold by: Amazon.com, LLC	$12.95

Shipping Address:
Eileen Feinman
10 Lincoln Pl
Port Washington, NY 11050-3221
United States

Shipping Speed:
Standard Shipping

Payment Information

Payment Method:
American Express | Last digits: 1002

Billing Address:
Eileen Feinman
10 Lincoln Pl
Port Washington, NY 11050-3221
United States

Item(s) Subtotal: $25.90
Shipping & Handling: $4.98

Total Before Tax: $30.88
Estimated Tax: $2.68

Grand Total:$33.56

To view the status of your order, return to Order Summary.

Please note: This is not a VAT invoice.

Page 1 of 1

Eileen Feinman

From: "Karen Whitaker" <whitaker_k@yahoo.com>
To: <reveileen@verizon.net>
Sent: Tuesday, August 25, 2009 11:45 AM
Subject: Thanks for your thanks!!!!!!!!!!

Dear Kailasvati,

We so enjoyed watching your card/video! Your thank you touched our hearts!

We love you guys!

Jyoti, Jivan, Kalavati and Tony

PS I was talking with Jivan recently about how much you appreciated his notepad he made for you, and he said he wanted to send you a letter. It said I think, "Dear Kailasvati, You and Ron can visit anytime. Jivan" We do love seeing you! He's been asking if you got it yet, and has expressed wanting to get a letter back in the mail from you. He'd love that if you would, if you get the chance!

8/31/2009